EPIC

Action and adventure collide in **EPIC**. Plunge into a universe of powerful beasts, hair-raising tales, and high-speed excitement. Astonishing explorations await. Can you handle it?

This edition first published in 2023 by Bellwether Media, Inc.

No part of this publication may be reproduced in whole or in part without written permission of the publisher. For information regarding permission, write to Bellwether Media, Inc., Attention: Permissions Department, 6012 Blue Circle Drive, Minnetonka, MN 55343.

Library of Congress Cataloging-in-Publication Data

LC record for Remote Control Cars available at: https://lccn.loc.gov/2022038237

Text copyright © 2023 by Bellwether Media, Inc. EPIC and associated logos are trademarks and/or registered trademarks of Bellwether Media, Inc.

Editor: Rachael Barnes   Designer: Josh Brink

Printed in the United States of America, North Mankato, MN.

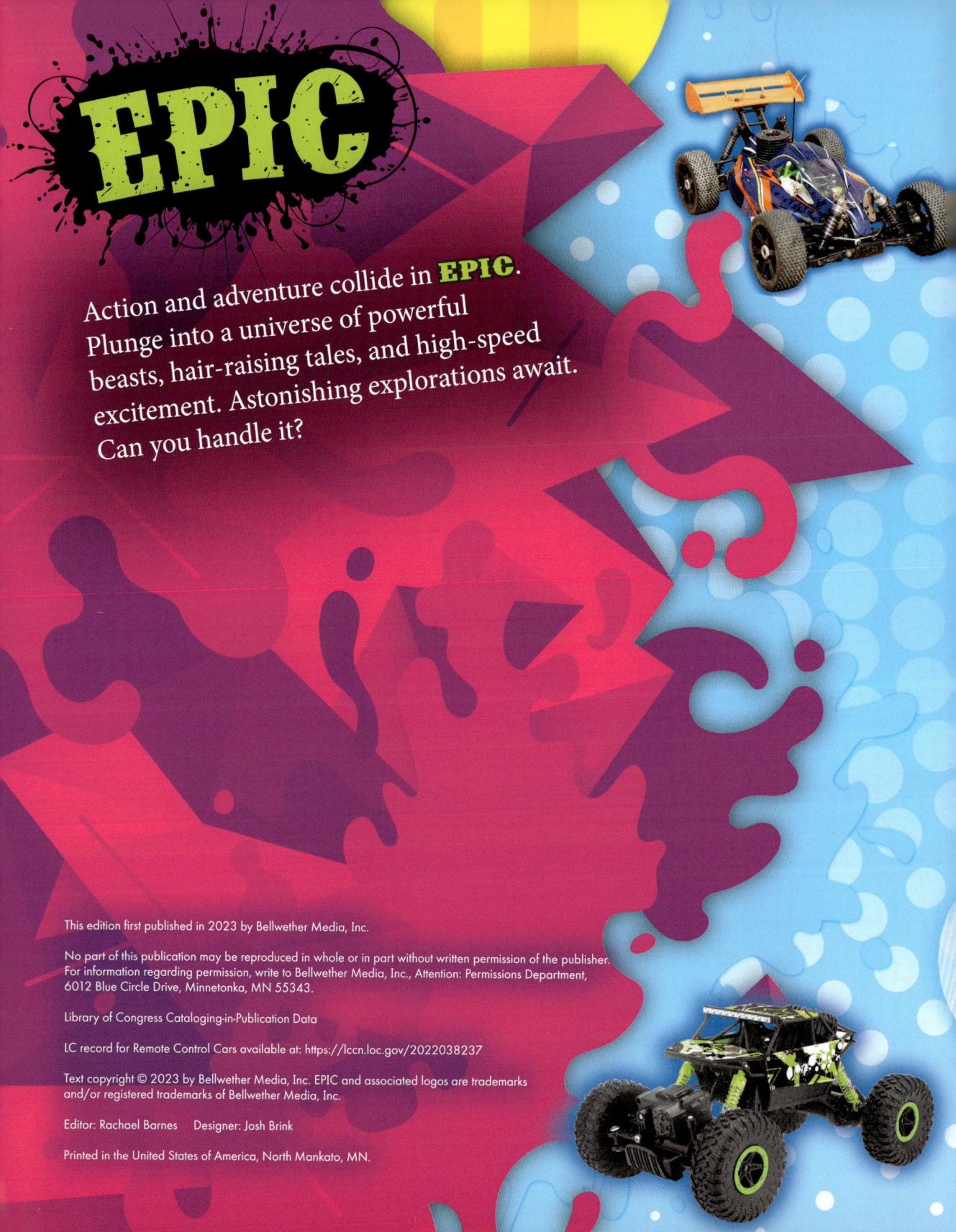

TABLE OF CONTENTS

Ready, Set, Race!....................4
The History of........................6
   Remote Control Cars
Remote Control Cars Today..14
More Than a Toy...................20
Glossary................................22
To Learn More......................23
Index....................................24

Ready, Set, Race!

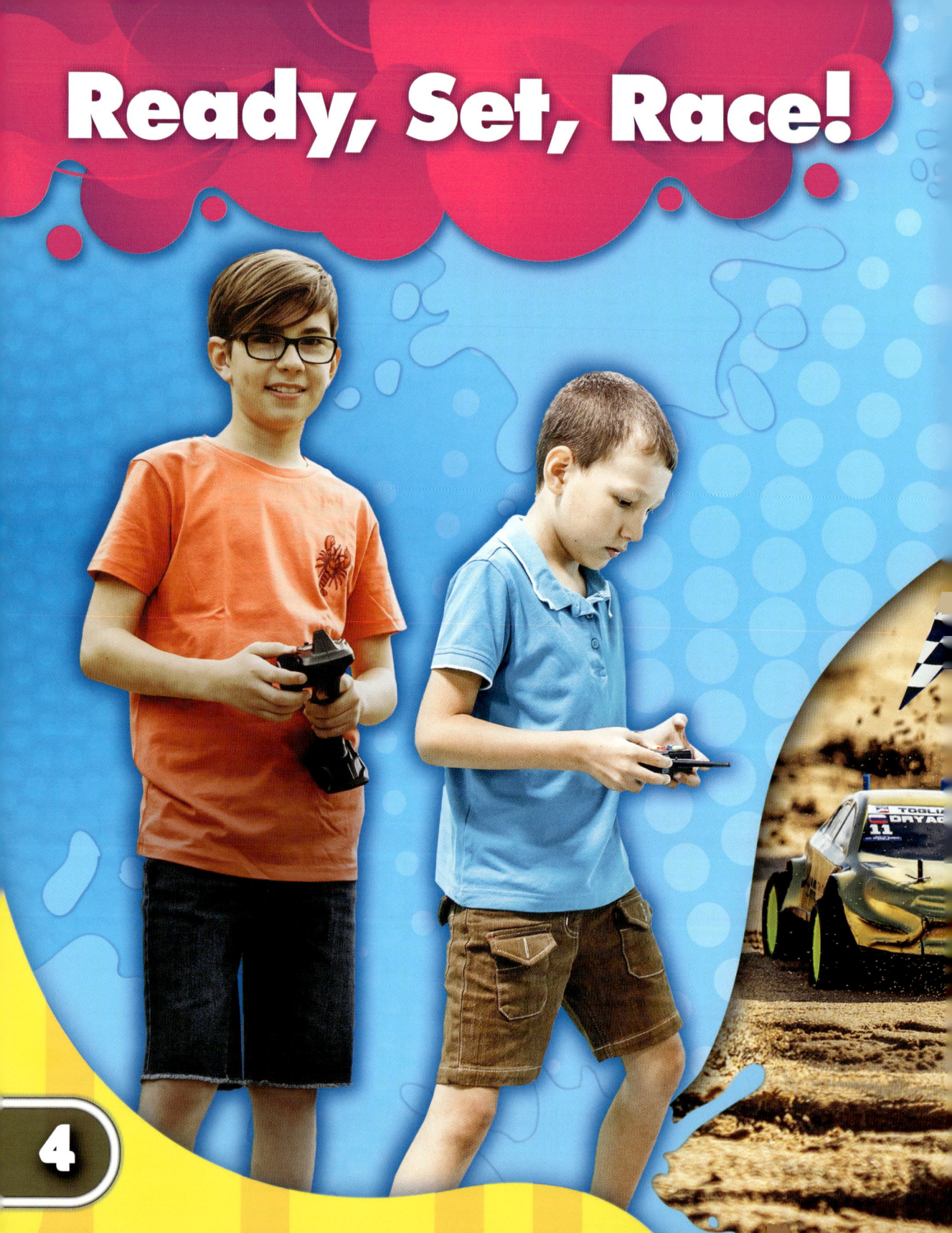

Two friends stand outside with **remote controls**. They are racing remote control cars!

Suddenly, one car speeds ahead. It crosses the finish line. The driver cheers as he wins the race!

The History of Remote Control Cars

Remote control cars, or RC cars, **debuted** in 1966. They were created in Italy by Elettronica Giocattoli. The first **model** was of the Ferrari 250LM sports car.

Soon, more companies began selling RC cars and build-your-own kits.

POWERED BY PLANES?

SOME EARLY RC CARS WERE MADE WITH ENGINES FROM MODEL AIRPLANES!

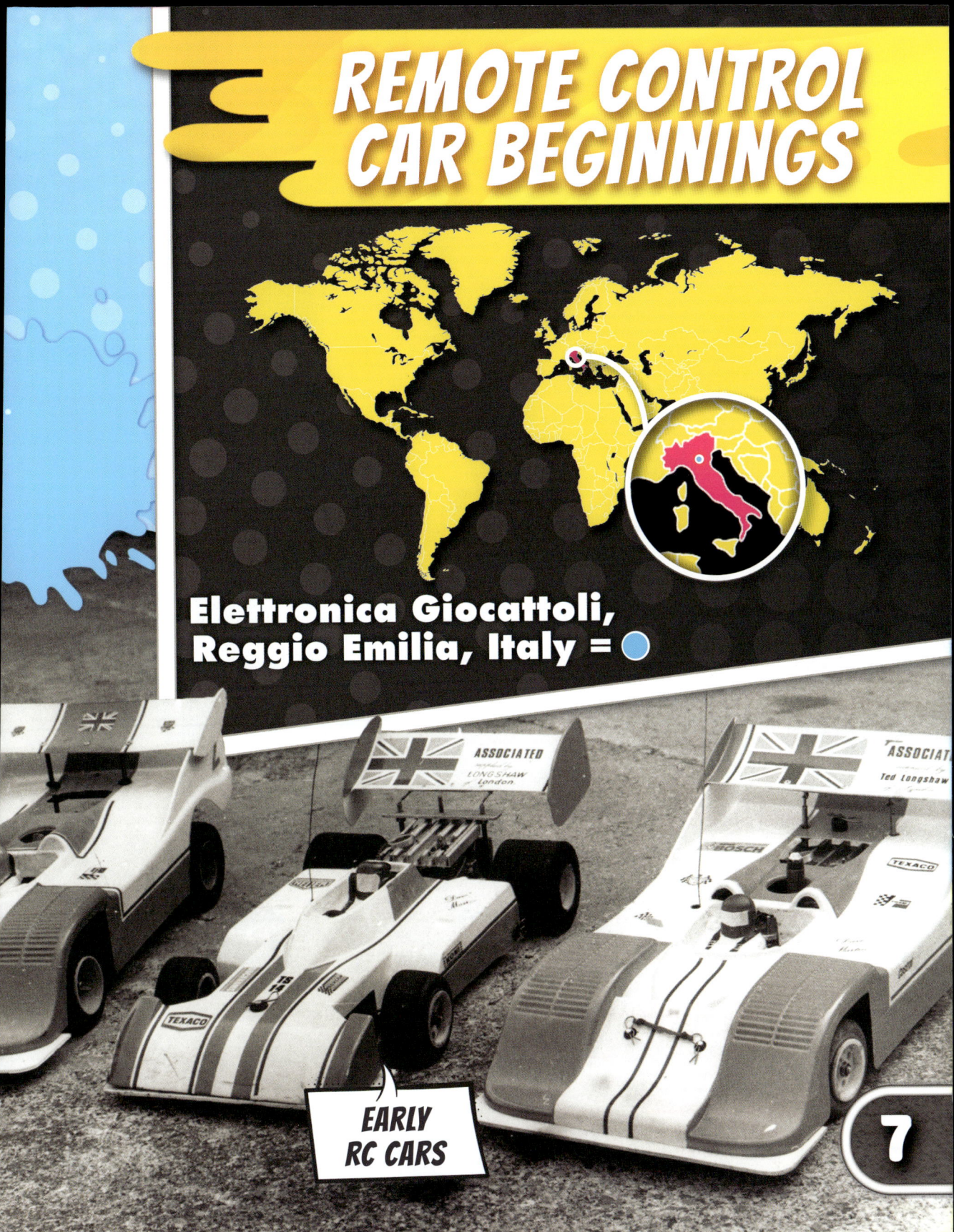

REMAKE OF AN EARLY OFF-ROAD RC CAR

More RC cars hit the road in the 1970s. Some RC cars were **electric**. Others were **nitro-powered**. The first **off-road** electric RC car was made in 1979.

Drivers formed RC car clubs. They made tracks and raced with friends!

ONE LARGE TRACK

THE WORLD'S LARGEST ALL-YEAR OFF-ROAD TRACK IS THE THORNHILL RACING CIRCUIT. THIS RC CAR TRACK COVERS AROUND 24,000 SQUARE FEET (2,230 SQUARE METERS)!

RC buggies became popular in the 1980s. The Team Associated RC10 was a favorite. It debuted in 1984.

TEAM ASSOCIATED RC10

BLACKFOOT MONSTER TRUCK

In 1986, the Blackfoot monster truck was released. It had a tough look! The kit was easy to build.

RC pan cars were a favorite in the 1990s. They were made for racetracks.

In 2004, RC rock crawlers became popular. These cars climbed rocky ground with ease!

ROCK CRAWLER

REMOTE CONTROL CAR TIMELINE

1966
Elettronica Giocattoli creates the first RC car

1979
The first off-road RC car is made

1984
Team Associated makes the RC10, one of the first RC cars made for racing

1990s
RC pan cars become favorite RC cars

2004
RC rock crawlers become popular

13

Remote Control Cars Today

There are many different RC cars! RC buggies, monster trucks, and rock crawlers drive off-road.

RC touring cars and pan cars zoom on racetracks. They often look like real cars!

REMOTE CONTROL CAR TYPES

buggy

monster truck

rock crawler

touring car

RC cars run in different ways. Some use gasoline or **solar power**. Electric RC cars often have **rechargeable batteries**.

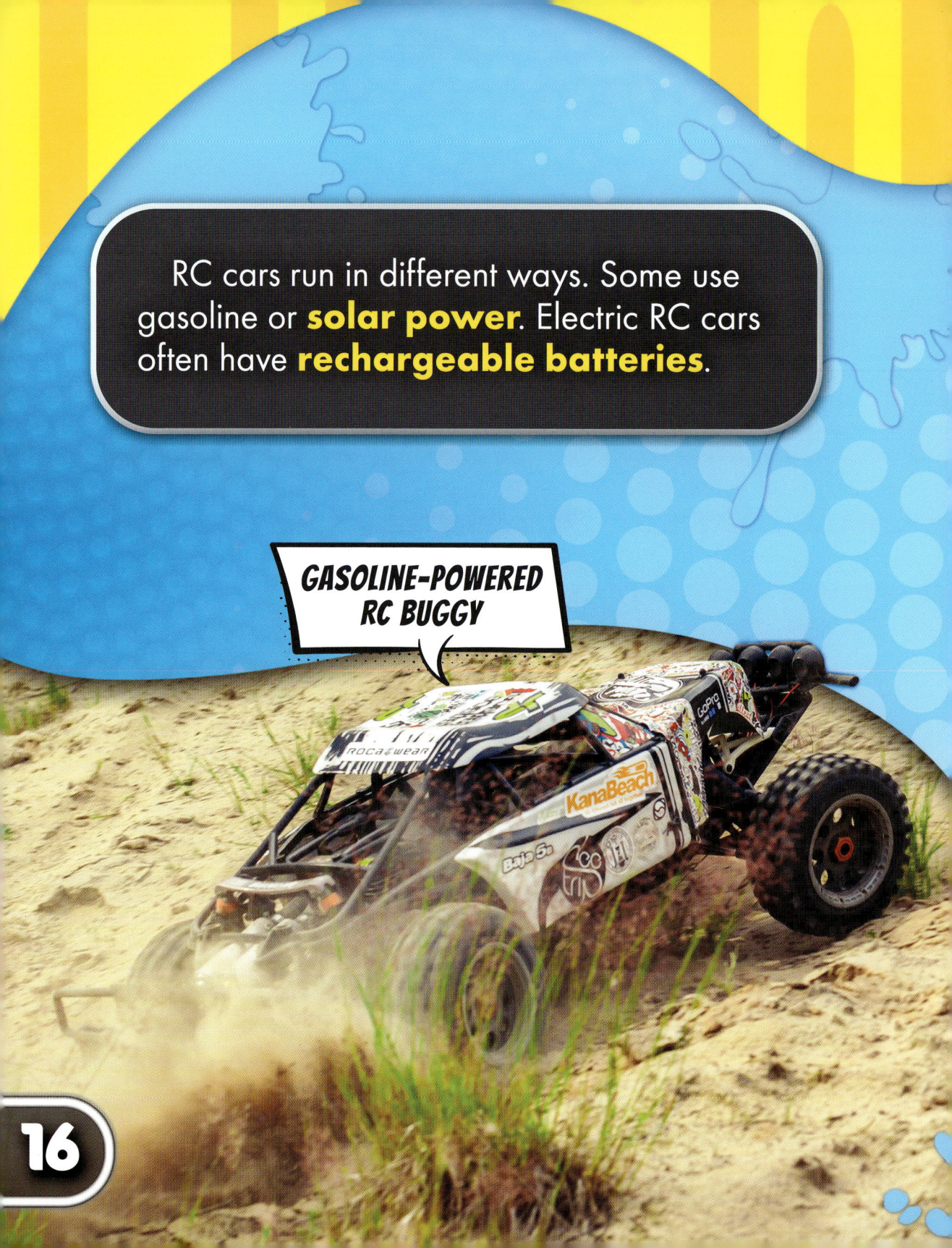

GASOLINE-POWERED RC BUGGY

A SPEEDING BULLET

THE FASTEST RC CAR IS THE "RADIO CONTROLLED BULLET." THIS BATTERY-POWERED CAR CAN REACH SPEEDS OF UP TO 202 MILES (325 KILOMETERS) PER HOUR!

Remote controls have also changed. Some RC cars are controlled by **smartphones**!

RC cars are fun for all ages! Kids and adults enjoy building RC cars from kits.

Some adults collect RC cars. Older cars can cost a lot of money!

More Than a Toy

RC car drivers still race in clubs. Some drivers race **professionally**!

Drivers also visit **conventions**. They meet other drivers and see the newest RC cars. RC cars bring people together!

RC EXPO PROFILE

What Is It? A convention for RC cars, RC airplanes, and drones

Where Is It? Pomona, California

When Does It Happen? Once a year

Glossary

conventions—events where fans of a subject meet

debuted—were shown to the public for the first time

electric—relating to electricity; electricity is a form of energy that is carried through wires and is used to power things such as machines and lights.

model—a small copy of something

nitro-powered—runs on a type of gas that has a chemical called nitrogen

off-road—used on trails or dirt roads

professionally—as a job or in a way that makes money

rechargeable batteries—batteries that can be reused

remote controls—devices that can control something else from a distance

smartphones—cell phones with advanced features such as internet access and apps

solar power—electricity that comes from the sun

To Learn More

AT THE LIBRARY

Higgins, Nadia. *Toys Then and Now*. Minneapolis, Minn.: Jump!, 2019.

Polinsky, Paige V. *Toy Cars*. Minneapolis, Minn.: Bellwether Media, 2023.

Ringstad, Arnold. *What's Inside a Remote-Controlled Car?* North Mankato, Minn.: The Child's World, 2019.

ON THE WEB

FACTSURFER

Factsurfer.com gives you a safe, fun way to find more information.

1. Go to www.factsurfer.com.
2. Enter "remote control cars" into the search box and click 🔍.
3. Select your book cover to see a list of related content.

Index

beginnings, 7
Blackfoot, 11
buggies, 10, 14, 16
clubs, 8, 20
collect, 19
conventions, 20
electric, 8, 16
Elettronica Giocattoli, 6, 7
Ferrari 250LM, 6
gasoline, 16
history, 6, 8, 10, 11, 12
Italy, 6, 7
kits, 6, 11, 18
model airplanes, 6
monster truck, 11, 14

nitro-powered, 8
off-road, 8, 9, 14
pan cars, 12, 14
Radio Controlled Bullet, 17
RC Expo, 21
rechargeable batteries, 16
remote controls, 5, 17
rock crawlers, 12, 14
solar power, 16
Team Associated RC10, 10
Thornhill Racing Circuit, 9
timeline, 13
touring cars, 14
tracks, 8, 9, 12, 14
types, 15

The images in this book are reproduced through the courtesy of: Cosmin Sava, cover (hero); Kaca Skokanova, cover (orange controller); abhinavmathurindia, cover (top right red RC car); Pelikh Alexey, cover (yellow Hummer); waller66, cover (middle left red RC car); JCDH, cover (blue and orange RC car), p. 2 (blue RC car); Purple Clouds, cover (yellow controller and orange RC car); Shyamalamuralinath, cover (bottom blue RC car); Jarp2, back cover (top left), p. 15 (buggy); FiledIMAGE, back cover (top right); PixieMe, back cover (bottom left); fotosv, back cover (bottom right); Mikhail Zyablov, p. 3 (green RC car); Audrius Merfeldas, p. 3 (red RC car); Shotmedia, p. 4 (child left); frantic00, p. 4 (child right); IVSHIN Ilia, p. 5 (RC cars); Joaquin Corbalan P, p. 5 (finish line); tomm/ Alamy, p. 6 (plane engine); Smith Archive/ Alamy, p. 7; Mark Benson/ flickr, p. 8; Mirrorpix/ Getty Images, p. 9; Associated Electrics, Inc., pp. 10, 13 (1984 fact); Alberto Massarotto, Ampro Engineering, p. 11; zulkeflyjalil, pp. 12-13; Monica Garza 73, p. 13 (2004 fact); Itrados, pp. 14-15; Nils Z, p. 15 (monster truck); Ryall Studios, p. 15 (rock crawler); Oleksandr Osipov, p. 15 (touring car); PuXa2, p. 16; picture alliance/ Getty Images, p. 17; stockphoto-graf, p. 18; OlegDoroshin, p. 19; 2windspa/ Getty Images, p. 20; Jordan Siemens/ Getty Images, p. 21; testing, p. 21 (red RC car); Art Konovalov, p. 22.